To: ——————————————————————

♡ Eph. 3:20

"Just Ask Joy . . ."

"Just Ask Joy . . ."

How to Be
Socially Savvy
in All Situations

"Just Ask Joy . . ."

How to Be
Socially Savvy
in All Situations

*Power Tips and Avoidable Faux Pas
for Business and Social Etiquette*

by Joy Weaver

"Just Ask Joy . . ."

How to Be Socially Savvy in All Situations
Power Tips and Avoidable Faux Pas
for Business and Social Etiquette

© 2005 Joy Weaver

Written by Joy Weaver

Manufactured in the United States.

For information, please contact:
Brown Books Publishing Group
16200 North Dallas Parkway, Suite 170
Dallas, Texas 75248
www.brownbooks.com
972-381-0009
A New Era in Publishing™

Paperback ISBN: 1-933285-20-6
LCCN 2005932767
1 2 3 4 5 6 7 8 9 10

Introduction

How do you know what you do not know? That question always comes up after I teach my protocol sessions. We are not born with manners—many of us never received training on real social skills from our parents when we were children, and colleges do not teach etiquette classes—then we get into the business world and just do the best we can.

Several years ago, I encountered the same feeling of "How could I not have known all this information—this long!" I was vice president of a national company in Dallas and, at the same time, was heading up a mentoring program that had asked me to speak to a group about manners. Take it from me—just because you have a good job does not mean you know the rules of etiquette. I took an etiquette class, and I had no idea that my life was about to change forever.

I became so interested in this area of personal development that I decided to take a leap of faith and start my own etiquette business—Protocol Enterprises. I wanted to receive professional training by the best, and I did. I first received training from the Leticia Baldridge Business Etiquette Program, and then I graduated from the Protocol School of Washington, D.C., receiving my certification as a Corporate Etiquette and International Protocol Consultant.

Since 2000, my company has thrived, and I am fortunate to work with some of the best companies in the nation. I develop programs that teach business and social skills to companies, nonprofit and civic groups, and individuals ranging from Fortune 500 executives to children, teenagers, and college groups. It is extremely rewarding for me to see individuals elevating their self-confidence and improving their chances to succeed through my specialized training. It is such a blessing to be paid for something I love to do.

Like it or not, we are constantly being evaluated based upon our social skills—how we speak, listen, and respond; our body language and dress; and the way we handle ourselves in the boardroom, while attending a wedding ceremony, or at the dining table. First opinions are many times formed long before we ever speak a word. The obvious question is, "What can I do about this situation?" The answer is simple—get serious about developing your personal, social, and professional skills, and you may improve your chances of advancing to the top. Etiquette training will help you no matter what your position is in life. Do not allow this one area to hold you back. You may have a wonderful education and many years of experience, but please realize that you need more than that. You need the self-esteem and self-confidence that come from knowing how to navigate through all situations you may encounter on a daily basis.

There are numerous etiquette books in the bookstore; many of these manner guides are large and detailed, so it can be difficult to find the quick answer you need to get you through the current situation you may be facing. Thus, I have written *Just Ask Joy… How to Be Socially Savvy in All Situations*, which is a book that contains the basic rules for social situations in simple lists so that you can find answers easily and grasp the basics that will enable you to be confident in a particular situation. It will just take a minute to pick the subject of choice and review the tip list and/or faux pas list. These lists will help equip you to go into business and social situations confidently.

I would love to hear from you. Please let me know if you too find yourself saying… *"I didn't know how much I didn't know!"*

— Joy Weaver

Acknowledgements

I want to give credit and honor to Jesus, my Lord and Savior, who has always provided a way for me. He allowed me—a little girl from West Texas—to grow up without my real parents in an area so rural that it took me an hour and a half to get to school. I went on to receive a Bachelor of Science degree, move to the big city, and land an amazing career helping others develop the skills that are beneficial to people at all stages in life.

Next, I want to thank my elderly aunt, Sally Wilson (who has gone to be with the Lord), for taking me in when I was only eighteen months of age. She had raised six children (who were all old enough to be my parents) and was ready for retirement, when my mother suddenly died of heart surgery complications, and my dad left to finish a career in the military. Sally Wilson, better known as "my mama," loved me and raised me as her own. I do not even want to think about where I might be now without her. We were not rich in possessions, but rich in love. She had me in church every time the doors were open, and she taught me the first lesson in etiquette—Luke 6:31: "Treat others the way you want to be treated."

Next, I want to acknowledge my wonderful husband, James, who has been a constant source of encouragement as I pursue my lifelong dreams. At the writing of this book, we have been married four years, but even while we were dating and I first shared with him my goals in life, he was quick to say, "Go for it—God has more in store for you than you could ever imagine." James is a very experienced businessman and has been extremely helpful in leading me in the right direction as my territories continue to expand.

I also want to thank my longtime prayer warriors who have been a constant source of encouragement: Cynthia, Charlotte, Bonnie, Lisa, Nina, Lynne, Katherine, Kara, Kay, and Kaye. I want to give special thanks to Robin and Tracie, who were instrumental in helping me with the development of my book—I could not have done it without them.

Finally, I want to thank you, my readers, for buying the book. I am honored to have the opportunity to be a small part of your life and to help as you develop into the person you want to be.

— Joy Weaver

Table of Contents

Part Six
Decisions, Decisions, Decisions . . .
Situations We Face on a Daily Basis

Part Seven
Growing up . . .
For Young Children and Young Adults

Part One

Just for Starters

Okay, let us get started with several of my most popular lists ...

* **My Personal Tips and Faux Pas**
  These are the basic principles I use to guide me
  through life.

* **Top Ten Etiquette Faux Pas**
  In my book I will share many faux pas on a variety
  of subjects, but these are my top ten.

* **Tech Etiquette**
  We have more technology available to us today than ever
  before in the history of mankind. With this increased
  technology comes a new and different way of living our lives
  and running our businesses—and an entirely new set of
  technological, social, and business rules to guide us.

My Personal Tips and Faux Pas

Here are some of my favorite personal tips and some of the faux pas I have learned in the ongoing lessons of life. I believe this knowledge will support you, no matter what season of your life you're in as you read this book. These are the basic principles I believe in now and try to follow as I make my journey through life. The remainder of the book is based upon well-researched etiquette rules. These rules are <u>fact</u> while the principles below are <u>opinion</u>.

Tips

* Follow the "Golden Rule": *Treat others the way you want to be treated.*

* Realize that success is measured by what you do, compared to what you are capable of doing.

* Understand that God's delays are not His denials.

* Believe that a life without prayer is a life without power.

* Hide God's word in your heart.

* Know that it is not necessarily the situation, but how the situation is handled, that matters.

* Behave your way to success.

* Realize that life is about choices.

* Alter your attitude, and you can alter your life.

* Learn that it is not where you start, but rather where you finish, that counts.

Faux Pas

✿ Waiting on the future instead of preparing for it.

✿ Trading what you want most for what you want now.

✿ Being afraid to stand up for what is right for fear of criticism.

✿ Blaming your past.

✿ Being lazy!

✿ Making a permanent decision based on a temporary storm.

✿ Getting back at others.

✿ Confusing class and money.

Top Ten Etiquette Faux Pas

In my book, you will receive tips and faux pas on a variety of subjects. This "Top Ten" list reveals some of the most common etiquette faux pas people commit on a daily basis. These faux pas will appear numerous times throughout the book:

1. Forgetting to turn cell phones on manner mode (silent/vibrate) in public places—and even worse, proceeding to answer calls with a "cell yell."

2. Not responding to party invitations—just showing up and bringing a friend.

3. Not sending a thank-you note or at least a thank-you e-mail.

4. Being late to meetings. This says that your schedule and time are more important than others' in the meeting.

5. Coughing and sneezing in your social (right) hand. Your right hand is your social hand, and your left hand is your personal hand. No one wants to shake hands with someone who has just coughed into his or her hand.

6. Re-gifting—it is wrong! If you do not like a gift you've been given, donate it or give it to someone who would use it—don't pass it off as a thoughtful gift you purchased for someone else!

7. Using the wrong bread plate or water glass—remember: **B.M.W.** (**B**read on the left, **M**eal in the center, **W**ater on the right).

8. Inviting someone to dinner and not paying—the person who invites, pays.

9. Applying lipstick at the table. All personal grooming should be done in the restroom.

10. Sending text messages or e-mails during meetings, worship services, weddings, or funerals.

Bonus Faux Pas—Using a toothpick, crunching ice, or chewing gum!

❧

> *We must give our best and be our best. How can we be our best if we don't know the basics?*

Tech Etiquette

ﮮ

If you are in the business world, or if you are a parent, a student, a socialite, a retired person, or basically if you are breathing in and out, you have witnessed one of the snafus listed below. Sending e-mails and text messages is extremely addictive, so if you catch yourself unable to refrain from any of the offensive behaviors listed, go ahead and check into a treatment center for dependent techie addicts.

Faux Pas

* Yakking in public on wireless cell phone headsets. (*Uh, are you talking to me or have you completely lost it? Oh! I see that you are talking into a wireless headset.*) Why not take your call to a private or semi-private area? Please do not make others have to listen to your side of a phone conversation. This screams, "I am self-centered and thoughtless."

* Oh, how cool—setting your ringer as loud as it will go so it will blare out "Sweet Home Alabama" or perhaps the voice of your sweet child screaming, "Daddy, you have a call!" You know who you are, so PLEASE, for the sake of the rest of our sanity, turn your cell phone down—even better, switch to manner mode.

* Text messaging during meetings, school classes, worship services, movies, dates, or any other private events such as weddings or funerals. You have to be kidding . . . text messaging at a funeral! Some people have no shame.

* Checking stock updates or sports scores on your cell phone while you are attending any of the aforementioned events.

❊ Overabbreviating. Text messaging is efficient unless the entire message is abbreviated (lol, brb, ty).

❊ Text messaging to ask for a date. Be a man and pick up the phone!!

❊ Instant messaging—it's distracting when the little window pops up constantly, or even worse, what if someone IMs you while you're away from your desk and the window is up on your screen for all to read? (This is a great reminder—never write anything you would not want a third party to read.)

❊ Taking unauthorized pictures of others with a cell phone camera—this invades their privacy. Even worse—posting the photographs on the Internet.

❊ Selfish blogging. If you are a blogger, remember to give as well as take information, and make sure not to plagiarize or offer your editing and proofreading services when no one has asked. Remember, it is much better to be a positive blogger than a negative one. If you do not like a blog, refrain from commenting.

❊ Conducting conversations in public while using walkie-talkie technology—keep the speaker function off and the conversations brief.

Part Two

Climbing the Corporate Ladder

The real difference-maker in our professional careers is not always our experience and education, but, in many cases, it is our ability to know how to navigate through life with grace and dignity. The following chapters will guide you through the various situations you may encounter as you travel through your professional career.

* Dress for Success—Men

* Dress for Success—Women

* "Ace Your Job Interview" Etiquette

* Business Meeting Etiquette

* Travel Tipping

* Jetiquette

* Dining Etiquette

* Conversation and Listening Etiquette

* Networking Skills Etiquette

* E-Mail Faux Pas

* Telephone and Voice Mail Etiquette

* Cubicle (Workplace) Etiquette

* Home Office Etiquette

Dress for Success—Men

First impressions are instant and long lasting. Fifty-five percent of a first impression is determined by the way we are dressed and groomed.

Tips

Grooming and other details:

* PLEASE pull the hair out of your ears (do not cut it—it will only look stubby), and trim the hair growing out of your nose—NOW!

* Remember, earrings are out of style for men. (It was a 90's thing!)

* You can wear cologne or aftershave, but keep in mind one word—*minimal.*

* Keep your eyes at a professional level. Do not look, glance, or stare at a woman's chest. Regardless of what you think, she can see you looking.

* Gross! Do not bite your nails, pick your nose, suck on your teeth, or scratch. (It is noticed!)

* Keep your hair stylish (and clean).

* Keep your fingernails trimmed and clean. (Real men get manicures.)

* Avoid wearing the Mr. T starter set—lose the multiple chains and rings. (One chain around your neck and one ring on each hand is acceptable.)

It is better to overdress than to underdress in all work environments—business, business casual, and casual.

Business Attire:

❋ Be aware that a dark-colored suit is perceived as professional (unless you are an Elvis impersonator).

❋ Remember, a long-sleeved starched shirt (preferably white) is a must. (The shirt cuff should extend slightly past your jacket sleeve.)

❋ Make sure your tie extends to the bottom of your belt. Cartoon characters on your ties take away all of your credibility. When in doubt, stick with stripes or polka dots.

❋ Men: match your shoes to your belt, and your socks to your pants.

❋ Remember this key rule: if you are expected to tie a tie, you should tie your shoes, too … in other words, the power shoe is a lace up.

❋ Please tell me you know by now, light-colored socks with a dark suit are hysterical, and what is even funnier … socks that are too short and expose your leg.

❋ Realize that Larry King is the only one who looks good in suspenders—but if you must, do not wear a belt also.

❋ Remember: button the top button on your jacket when you stand, and unbutton it when you sit down.

❋ If you wear an overcoat, make sure the sleeves are long enough to cover the suit coat and shirtsleeves.

Business Casual:
(*Always know the company's dress policy.*)

❊ Business casual requires no tie, normally. If you are going to a function that calls for business casual and you are unsure of your host's policy, never hesitate to make a call and ask; otherwise, wear a tie. You can always remove it later—better safe than sorry!

❊ Keep dark slacks and a solid-colored shirt at the top of the professional list for business casual.

❊ Consider a khaki pant with a solid shirt or a pullover as a good alternative. (Avoid shirts with loud prints.)

❊ Keep in mind that business casual shoes are normally slide-on (dress) shoes (not sandals or topsiders).

❊ Wear socks and match them to your pants.

❊ Know that wrinkles are unacceptable.

Casual:
(*Always know the company's dress policy.*)

❊ You are always safe with khaki, navy, or some other basic-colored slacks.

❊ Wear either short- or long-sleeved shirts, preferably with collars.

❊ You can wear shirts that are colorful, but not tropical or neon.

❁ Jeans may be acceptable in many companies on casual Friday. If this is the case with your organization, avoid the trendy grunge look, the low hip-hugger style, and the "run over by a lawn-mower" trend. These are not professional by any stretch of the imagination.

❁ You can wear most casual shoes, but definitely no tennis shoes.

❁ It is always good to know that khaki walking shorts may be acceptable for certain summertime outdoor activities.

❁ Remember: your personal style is not only dictated by what you wear, but also by your conduct and how you carry yourself. They go hand in hand—like a matching belt and shoes.

Dress for Success—Women

Just as unpredictable as the weather, women's fashion trends are in a constant state of flux. As the saying goes, "If you don't like it, just wait a while; it'll change." While many of the fashion commandments of the past are now passé, by no means do we live in a fashion free-for-all. Appropriateness is the key for every situation, and while trends come and go, the basic rules remain rather constant.

Tips

Common and not-so-common sense grooming tips and other details:

❊ Remember, if you can look down and see cleavage, so can everyone else—it is your choice.

❊ Wear the style that looks best on you, and no matter what, keep up to date with the styles, but do not worry about the trendy trends.

❊ Wear white after Labor Day only if you want to "take a walk on the wild side." While trends of fashion might say that it is okay to wear bright white between Labor Day and Easter, the rules of etiquette remain in place—winter white is still the only white that is acceptable during this time of the year. (While we are on the subject, ditch the white shoes during winter.)

❊ Keep in mind this important tip about makeup: your face should not be darker than your neck, and vice versa. Change makeup colors as your skin changes colors throughout the year.

❋ Wear a minimal amount of perfume and consider wearing it only after five p.m. More people than you think are allergic to perfume, and most do not agree on scents.

❋ Smokers—face it! You cannot cover up the cigarette smoke smell with perfume or cologne. Non-smokers can smell that combo coming a mile away—eww!

❋ Please know that tattoos and ear piercing above the lobe are tacky. If you go for a real job interview, remember to cover both.

❋ Yes—you can now wear gold and silver jewelry together; however, like anything else, too much of a good thing is bad. Remember: one ring per hand, and if you have on a pair of fabulous earrings, do not wear a necklace, and vice versa.

❋ Nails (hands and toes) must look good at all times. This is not an option!

❋ Mustaches are not normal for women—make an appointment to get a lip wax. While you are there, have a brow wax also!

❋ Many agree when I say, *"The taller the hair, the closer to God."* However, big hair went out of style twenty years ago (along with chocolate lip liner), so refrain from "the tease and freeze" trend of the coveted 70s and 80s.

❋ Remember that panty lines are tacky.

❋ Wear gloves and look fabulous—but it is a faux pas, no matter how cold your hands, not to remove gloves before shaking hands.

❀   I hope you are one of the lucky women who can wear hats—*more power to you!* Wear them indoors and outdoors at any time of the night or day. Remember, an evening hat or cocktail hat, which is smaller in size, is worn after six p.m. Also, refrain from wearing big hats to an event where others have to sit behind you and look forward—like movies, weddings, or worship centers.

Business Attire:
(*Know your company's dress policy.*)

❀   If you have an interview or an important meeting, you cannot go wrong with a darker-colored suit and a lighter-colored tailored or silk blouse.

❀   If you wear a suit, do not wear flats. You must wear a heel, even if it is a small heel.

❀   Belts, shoes, and handbags no longer have to match—but they should coordinate.

❀   Mini boots must not be worn with skirts.

❀   Make sure your shoes are in good condition. Replace tips on heels as soon as you hear the first "click."

❀   Throw away all white panty hose—choose a neutral tone.

❀   Be careful—mixing and matching suits can be disastrous. Make sure you coordinate the entire outfit, and always look in a full-length mirror before leaving home.

Business Casual:
(Know your company's dress policy.)

❀ Dress professionally, yet relaxed—possibly a sweater set (in place of blazers) with slacks or skirts.

❀ You can wear flat-soled shoes as an option, but flip-flops are not business casual—no matter how expensive or popular they may be!

❀ Only wear casual dress on the weekends—never to work.

❀ Remember, capri pants, sleeveless shirts, flip-flops, jeans, warmups, and shorts are all very casual clothes. If you need to run into work for two seconds on your day off and you are dressed casually, how would an outside client know it is your day off? Any time you are at your place of business, dress the part!

Never underestimate the power of your appearance.

ϒ

> *First impressions are made in the first five seconds. Your dress and body language speak volumes about you even before you say a word.*

"Ace Your Job Interview" Etiquette

ᴥ

Follow these tips and they will greatly increase your chances of landing that very important position you have been working so hard for all your life.

Tips

* Make a great first impression. It is "showtime!" Proper dress and a proper handshake speak volumes. Be polished, stand up straight, smile, make good eye contact, and have a firm handshake. Also, remember you are being interviewed by the receptionist. Seven out of ten times, the interviewer will ask the receptionist about his or her first impression of you.

* Arrive early and follow the leader. Always arrive ten minutes early to the interview. (However, if you discover you are going to be late, call to explain the situation.) Know exactly where you are going, even if you have to scout out the location a day in advance. Remember to take a seat after you are asked, and let the interviewer take the lead in asking questions.

* Do your homework. Research and be knowledgeable about the company before the interview. Preparing several specific company questions shows your interest and confirms that you have done your homework. You must have accurate and updated resume materials. Make sure your telephone numbers are accurate and you have a professional message on your voice mail. Send a handwritten note on professional stationery, and e-mail a thank-you note immediately.

❋ Listen and be successful. Listening is the number one communication skill executives are seeking. You must be able to handle silence and avoid rambling—stay focused and make notes of questions you want to ask. Give the interviewer your undivided attention. Body language and nonverbal communication speak louder than words.

❋ Turn off your cell phone and pager! It will be embarrassing and unacceptable if your cell phone or pager rings during your interview. (And for Pete's sake, do not answer it if it does ring.)

Business Meeting Etiquette

Do not allow your business meetings to be a big waste of time. Follow these rules and make your meetings productive, yet enjoyable.

Tips

❋ Start and end the meeting on time, and follow the agenda.

❋ Always wait to be seated, allowing the person leading the meeting to make the decision on the proper seating arrangement.

❋ The leader should summarize all decisions made in the meeting, making sure everyone understands his or her responsibilities.

❋ Always turn your cell phone off or leave it on manner mode. Never take a call or check to see who is calling while you're in an important meeting.

❋ Show your respect by paying attention to the person who has the floor.

❋ Treat all information you receive in a meeting as confidential. Never try to be a know-it-all by sharing confidential information with others.

❋ Before making your presentation, always check the electronic equipment to make sure it works properly. Failure to do so could result in a disaster for you.

Avoid these issues when planning and attending a meeting.

Faux Pas

❋ Being late indicates to others that you think your time is more important than theirs.

❋ Using your PDA during the meeting shows others your lack of interest in the discussions.

❋ Chewing gum or crunching ice is something you should never do; it is very rude and distracting.

❋ Interrupting others or speaking out of turn shows disrespect for others in the meeting.

❋ Being an uninvited guest is rude. You should not attend a meeting unless you are specifically invited.

❋ Dominating the meeting by talking too much or by sidetracking the focus of the meeting is not acceptable.

❋ Arguing your point is a no-no. Do not be defensive if others do not agree with you.

Travel Tipping Etiquette

ولع

It appears that every business establishment you encounter has a tip jar. Here is a guide to assist you in knowing when and how much to tip.

Spring and summer are the times when many people travel for pleasure, and any vacation can be enhanced by receiving great service. The tips people give while traveling can make the difference between good service and great service, but many times, people are confused about whom to tip, when to tip, and the appropriate amounts to tip.

The word "tip" is an acronym for "To Insure Promptness." Remember, the amount of the tip is always based upon the level of customer service.

To help clear up the confusion and encourage proper tipping that results in outstanding service, you should follow these specific guidelines.

Tips

* **Train Station/Airport: Porter or Skycap.** Tip a minimum of two dollars per bag. Tip more if the bags are heavy. One to two dollars extra for curbside check-in is optional. You are not expected to tip flight attendants during the flight. Tip three to five dollars for wheelchair assistance, and if the person goes out of his or her way, tip more.

❁ **Ground Transportation.** Taxi, limo, or van driver—tip 15 percent of the total fare. Driver of courtesy shuttle—tip two dollars per traveler and more if the driver helps with bags. Valet or parking attendant—tip two to five dollars when the car is returned to you. It is not necessary to tip for dropping off the car, but always tip when picking it up for departure. Some car services include gratuity in the fee, so make sure the tip is not included beforehand.

❁ **Emergency Roadside Service.** Consider the level of danger and the difficulty of the repair. Tip an additional amount if it is roadside service versus in the safety of a parking lot. Towing service—tip five to twenty dollars depending upon circumstances and your desperation. Jump start—tip five to ten dollars. Tire change—tip five to ten dollars. Locked out of car—tip five to ten dollars.

Hotels:

❁ **Doorman.** Tip two dollars for hailing a cab, two to three dollars for help with your bags in or out of the car, and three to five dollars per bag for bringing bags to your room.

❁ **Bellman.** If the bellman just carries the bags to the front desk and then disappears, save the tip for the person who carries the bags to your room. When the bellman brings your bags to your room or from your room when you check out, tip three dollars per bag. Tip more for additional services.

❁ **Concierge.** Tip five to ten dollars for help with hard-to-get dinner reservations or theater tickets. Tipping is optional for recommendations. Tipping the concierge should be done at the time of service.

❋ **Room Service.** If gratuity is included on your check, no additional tip is required. If it is not included, add 15–20 percent to the total charge, depending on level of service. If you request extra pillows or an iron, tip a minimum of two dollars.

❋ **Maid Service.** Tip one to three dollars per day. Tip daily because there might be a different maid each day. Leave the tip on your pillow or in an envelope labeled "housekeeping."

❋ **IT Support Staff.** Tip five dollars for computer setup and help.

❋ **Restaurants: Maitre d'.** Tip ten dollars for a special table, complicated reservations, or a large party. Coat check—tip two dollars per coat. Wine sommelier—tip 8 to 10 percent of wine bill. Bartender—tip one dollar per drink. Wait person—tip 15 to 20 percent of total bill (the busing staff receives a portion). Restroom attendant—tip one dollar.

❋ **Spas, Salons, Barbers, Manicures, or Facials.** Normally, tip 15 percent. Massage therapist—tip 15 percent. Salon or spa package—determine in advance whether a service charge is included. If none is included, then tip 10 to 20 percent, split among the service providers. You can ask for it to be divided, pay each person at the time of service, or leave it in envelopes available at the front desk. Barber—tip 15 to 20 percent. Hair stylist—tip 15 to 20 percent. Shampoo—tip two to five dollars. Shoeshine—tip two to five dollars. A salon question asked over and over is: "Should I tip the owner of a salon, or is it considered an insult?" Melissa Renee, owner of MK Salon in Dallas, erases this old adage—"It is simple: tipping is up to the client's discretion. Tipping the stylist should always be based upon service, not tenure or ownership."

❋ **Cruise Ships.** Find out in advance what the tipping policy is for the ship. If you are supposed to tip, ask if it is done at the end of the trip or at the time of service. Oftentimes, at the end of the cruise, passengers are provided envelopes with suggested tip amounts. If you are supposed to tip, budget at least twenty dollars per day for all of the service employees: waiter—five dollars per day per person; cabin steward—five dollars per day per person; bus boy—two dollars per day per person; maitre d'—not necessary unless special services provided; bar steward—usually, 15 percent is automatically added to bill; baggage handlers/porters—two dollars per bag.

❋ **Tour Guides.** Check ahead to determine if the tip is included. If not, give 10 to 15 percent of the tour price.

Jetiquette

When we are fortunate enough to fly on a private plane, there are specific rules we must follow . . . if we want a return invitation!

Tips

* Do not be late! The plane will be drinking fuel at a rate you do not even want to know about, and being late is very inconsiderate to others, especially the owners.

* It should go without saying, but here goes anyway—don't bring a guest or a pet without the owner's prior consent.

* Travel light! If you are instructed to bring *only one bag*, that means *only one bag*. Weight and space are always a concern.

* Ask where to sit—in a private plane the owner has a favorite place to sit, and depending on the size of the plane, the pilot will make sure the weight is properly distributed.

* Turn down the sound! If you are listening to music, watching a movie, or playing a video game, make sure it is not vibrating or echoing outside your headphones.

* Refrain from wearing cologne or perfume—you will be in close quarters for a length of time, so why take a chance on your new French perfume choking those around you or perhaps flaring up someone's allergies?

* Pick up your own litter—just like your mom taught you. Leave the place better than you found it.

❋ Ask the owner or the person who rented the plane if you can contribute to the expense.

❋ Write a thank-you note to the owners immediately afterward to express your appreciation.

Bonus Tip—Bring a small gift to the owner to express your appreciation.

Dining Etiquette

Pay close attention to these situations if you want to leave a good impression at the dining table. Your dining etiquette will tell others much about you.

Tips

* When leaving the table, always push your chair back to the table.

* Pass food to the right when eating with a group.

* Place your napkin in your lap with the folded edge facing you.

* Place your napkin in the chair seat when leaving the table with plans to return.

* Never place your napkin on the table until you are leaving, and then place it to the left of your plate.

* Place butter on your bread plate and then spread it on your roll, one bite at a time. It is appropriate to open a hot roll and butter it immediately.

* Be considerate of others around you by using your "manners voice."

* When possible, you should be seated from the left side of the chair and exit from the right side.

* A properly trained wait person will serve your meal to you from your left and pick it up from your right.

❊ If you are eating at a buffet, wait for at least one or two people to be seated before you start eating.

❊ When ordering off the menu, wait until everyone has been served before you start eating.

❊ It is perfectly acceptable to ask the waiter for recommendations from the menu.

❊ Excellent service and large tips go hand in hand.

Faux Pas

❊ Making others nauseous by talking with a full mouth.

❊ Sticking an armpit in someone's face by reaching across the table instead of asking him to pass the dish.

❊ Taking a first bite before everyone has been served or before the host/hostess takes his or her first bite.

❊ Reverting to childhood by cutting your meal into bite-size pieces, instead of cutting one bite at a time.

❊ Eating too fast instead of pacing yourself with your companions.

❊ Putting used utensils back on the table, or hanging the knife and fork off your plate like paddles on a rowboat. Utensils should be placed in the resting position on the plate.

❊ Passing the salt and pepper separately, or passing with your hands on the top of the containers.

❊ Eating a roll the way you eat an apple instead of tearing off and buttering one bite at a time.

* Eating your neighbor's salad or drinking her water. Remember **B.M.W.**—**B**read to the left, **M**eal in the center, and **W**ater to the right.

* Putting on lipstick or other makeup at the table. All personal grooming should be reserved for the restroom.

* Being rude to the waiter and other wait staff—this shows lack of class and tells much about who you really are.

   Bonus faux pas—Using a toothpick or chewing gum in public!

Conversation and Listening Etiquette

Here are some successful habits you should develop to enhance your conversation and communication skills.

Tips

* Sincerely listen—pay attention when others are talking; it tells others that you are truly interested in them.

* Pay compliments—this is a great way to get a conversation started and make someone feel good. There is something special about everyone—it is our job to find it out and make that person feel special.

* Remember names. When you forget others' names, this tells them they are not that important to you.

* Maintain eye contact—it is rude to look away when someone is talking to you.

* Remember common interests so you can reference them in future conversations.

* Exhibit positive body language—this speaks volumes regarding how you really feel about what the other person is telling you.

* Always be up to date on current events to use in conversation—this gives you something to discuss other than yourself.

❊ Do not interrupt or monopolize the conversation. Refrain from telling long stories or dragging out details. Remember, when telling a story, have an interesting introduction, a strong closing, and make sure they are close together!

❊ Follow up! Follow up! Follow up! This is the key to building relationships with others.

Be just as enthusiastic about the successes of others as you are about your own.

Networking Skills Etiquette

Life is about relationships—the rest is just details! Like it or not, we must develop these basic skills in order to develop stronger and more productive relationships.

Tips

❋ *Note to self*: networking events are not about free food and drink. Many companies cannot figure out why their associates are not bringing in new business at networking events. Often, it is because employees huddle up and catch up on what is going on in their own company rather than networking with potential clients.

❋ Dress appropriately—a bad first impression is hard to overcome.

❋ Wear name tags on the right side. Print your first and last name large enough so others can read it at a glance.

❋ Learn how to make small talk, and remember: the key to success in networking is to get others talking about themselves.

❋ Get out of your comfort zone, and introduce yourself to others.

❋ Always remember these two words: BREATH MINTS! (Not chewing gum!) Bad breath will ruin any chance of a good first impression. Chewing gum says you are adolescent.

❋ Keep your drink in your left hand so when shaking hands, your right hand will not be cold and wet.

❋ Always be up to date on current events so you can easily start or add to conversations.

❋   Sincerely listen when the other person is talking. Look him or her in the eye, and occasionally nod your head to show that you are into the conversation.

❋   Smile sincerely and pay heartfelt compliments—nobody likes lip service!

❋   Make proper introductions. Remember, in business, everyone is a Martian—gender does not play a role. Persons of lesser authority are introduced to persons of greater authority, regardless of gender.

❋   Be ready to reintroduce yourself to someone who appears to have forgotten your name, and never hesitate to ask someone his or her name in the event you have forgotten it. Repeat it back in conversation once and write it down later, along with something of interest about this person. Perhaps he or she plays golf or likes to travel. Now you have a topic of conversation the next time you meet.

❋   Maintain eye contact (not a stare down) with the person to whom you are talking. Certainly do not glance at body parts, the television behind his or her head, or other people walking past you.

❋   Always remember to have business cards with you, but never go to an event with the intention of handing out a card to everyone you meet. Be selective in giving out your cards.

❋ Look at someone's business card with interest, and treat it with care. Never grab it and toss it into your handbag or coat pocket in front of the person who gave it to you. Always say "thank you," and tuck the card into a safe place so you can add it to your contact list later. Follow up your conversation with an e-mail or note card.

❋ Be approachable and maintain a sense of humor!

> *Everybody knows something*
> *I need to know . . . it is my job*
> *to figure it out!*

E-Mail Faux Pas

E-mails play an important role in our daily lives. We need to avoid these faux pas if we want to be effective with our e-mail communication.

* Answering e-mails while you are on the telephone with someone else. The person on the phone can hear you typing and can tell you are distracted.

* Using all UPPERCASE. (THIS MEANS YOU ARE SCREAMING!)

* Not using spell check before sending the e-mail. (Poor spelling is unacceptable.)

* Not replying back to a business e-mail within twenty-four hours. (At least let the sender know you received the e-mail.)

* Sending an e-mail when you are upset. (Wait until the next day—your attitude about the situation will likely change.)

* Forwarding junk mail. (Stop it!)

* Sending long, wordy e-mails as opposed to brief and concise e-mails. (Your reader will more likely respond to your e-mail if it is shorter.)

* Leaving off the subject line. (Give a heads-up on what's coming down the pike.)

* Replying to all. (Oops! How embarrassing!)

* Using a fancy font that no one can read. (A big faux pas.)

Telephone and Voice Mail Etiquette

Eighty-seven percent of our message is perceived through our voice and only 13 percent by our actual words. Our personality and mannerisms are revealed through the tone of our voice.

Tips

* _Always_ identify yourself before asking to speak to someone: "Hello, this is Joy Weaver. May I speak to Denise Waldrop?"

* Always ask for permission and wait for a response before putting someone on hold.

* Use call waiting wisely. If you are on the phone with someone and are expecting an important call, let your current caller know in advance so he or she will be prepared for the interruption.

* Realize, many people are not awake/coherent before seven a.m. or after ten p.m., so be respectful and make calls within these hours.

* We sometimes dial the wrong number. Do not just hang up in the other person's ear—apologize for the inconvenience.

* Use your normal voice and speak clearly. Remember, just because the person on the other end of the line is miles away does not mean you have to shout.

* Do not continue typing e-mails or doing other work when talking on the phone—this can be distracting and annoying to the other person.

❈   Do not assume that people will recognize your voice; be courteous and tell them who is calling.

❈   Avoid using this type of faux pas voice mail: "You have reached *the desk of* John Smith." (No one wants to leave a message for John's desk.)

❈   When leaving someone a voice mail message—make it brief and concise, and always leave a callback number!

❈   Make certain the answering message on your telephone gives brief but valuable information. "Hello, this is Joy Weaver. I will be out of my office today but will be checking my voice mail at three p.m. and will return your call at that time. If you have an emergency, you can contact me on my cell at 972-999-7777."

Cubicle (Workplace) Etiquette

When we work in an "open" environment (with cubicles for offices) it is most important, for the sanity and productivity of fellow associates, to be courteous and follow some simple guidelines.

Tips

* Refrain from barging in and starting a conversation without first asking permission.

* Use your "manners voice" at all times. Loud conversations are distracting to others.

* Avoid lengthy personal calls. Your neighbor may not be interested in the details of last night's hot date or your recent family reunion. Keep your personal conversations to a minimum.

* Do not conduct conference calls at your workstation—they are very distracting to others around you.

* Find an enclosed office or conference room if you need to have a meeting.

* Certainly you understand that not everyone enjoys the same music, so if your company allows you to listen to music at the office, keep it so low only you can hear it.

* Avoid using screen savers that make noise.

* Remember when you are eating at your workstation that your food may not smell as good to others as it does to you.

* Do not wear strong perfume, cologne, or aftershave—it can cause allergies in others around you or give them a headache.

❊ It is polite to switch your phone to voice mail when you are away from your workstation. This way your telephone does not ring excessively.

❊ Turn the volume down on the sound of new e-mails arriving.

❊ Make sure your workstation leaves a good impression—keep it neat, clean, and organized.

❊ Do not crunch on ice or eat hard candy at your workstation— unless you want to drive others crazy.

❊ Communicate with your neighbors and establish the "ground rules for harmony."

Home Office Etiquette

The corporate landscape is changing from long commutes and cubicles to convenient and cozy home offices. But working at home requires discipline and professionalism. While it is no longer a stigma to say you are working out of your home, it is crucial that you leave your customers and clients with the impression that they are dealing with a professional.

Faux Pas

* Allowing your pet to make sounds. If you are on a business call and your dog is barking in the background, it will destroy your professional image.

* Snacking secretly. It is easier to have snacks at your home office desk, so do not be tempted to have a little snack or crunch on ice while talking on a conference/business call.

* Crying babies or screaming children. This too will destroy your professional image when you try to carry on a business call— you will not be taken seriously by the person on the other end of the phone. Plan your business call while the kids are away or napping.

* Watching *Oprah!* Turn the TV or radio on mute while you're on a business/conference call.

* Performing household chores. Refrain from doing the laundry or loading the dishwasher during a business call. Your audience can hear every move you make on the other end of the line. *PLEASE*, do not even try to sneak in a bathroom break during a call—you might as well flush your professional image good-bye.

❀ Using a family voice mail message. A professional message is as essential as a separate business phone number at your home.

❀ "Whaz'up?" Allowing little ones or teenagers to answer your business line will leave a bad impression on your business caller. Limits must be established for your home office telephone. Explain "professionalism" and the importance of your children not answering your phone.

❀ Having call waiting on your phone. This is a dead giveaway that you are on a home phone and do not have a professional home office setup. It is best to have a business line that sends another caller into a second line or directly into voice mail. Do not allow the home phone to ring continuously while you are on the other line.

❀ Forgetting to use the mute button. If you are on a conference/business call, use the mute button on your telephone if you should need to have a side conversation.

❀ Playing music for everyone. Make sure your hold button does not play music when using it during a conference call.

❀ Giving your home address as your business address. If possible, leave "drive" or "avenue" off your business address. It is best to rent a P.O. box, which will give a professional appearance and offer personal security and privacy. Remember, also for safety reasons, you should avoid putting your home address on your Web site.

❀ Ringing doorbells. Turn the volume down on your doorbell so that it does not sound like "Avon calling" to your client on the other end of the line.

❈ Using an improper office setup. Set up your office in a separate part of your home, and develop a mindset that this is your place of business and treat it as such.

❈ Wearing pajamas and fuzzy slippers. Working at home, you may find it easy to wear your pajamas to the office. Go ahead and get dressed; it helps you get into the work mode.

❈ Losing power. Be prepared for technical failures/power outages, and have phone numbers handy in case you need prompt help.

❈ Not receiving your faxes. Many home offices have the same fax number and office number; make sure to switch the fax machine over when you are expecting a fax.

How do you know what you don't know?

Part Three

Being the Right Date and the Right Mate

Whether it is dating, dining, weddings, or proms, we are always more comfortable if we know what is expected of us. To polish up the rough edges, practice the simple but important guidelines outlined in the following chapters:

* Dating Etiquette

* Tips a Lady Should Know

* Tips a Gentleman Should Know

* Homecoming and Coming Home Etiquette

* Breakup Etiquette

* Wedding Etiquette

* Tips for Wedding Party Etiquette

* Wedding Ring Etiquette

* Anniversary Etiquette

Dating Etiquette

Follow these tips and definitely avoid these faux pas of dating . . . that is, if you want to increase your chances of a second date.

Tips

❋ Be on time. Not early, but on time. You do not want to give the impression that something is more important than your date.

❋ Pay if you are the one who gave the invitation. If a lady invites a gentleman on a date, it would be her responsibility to pay; however, a true gentleman should always offer.

❋ Silence your cell phone and turn off your PDA. Your date deserves your complete attention.

❋ Talk about something other than yourself. Being a good listener makes you extremely attractive.

Faux Pas

❋ Waiting until the last minute to invite someone on a date, make reservations, or purchase tickets.

❋ Being rude with your food: do not talk with your mouth full, eat too fast, or ask, "Are you going to eat all of that?"

❋ Being afraid to say "no." This applies to accepting the date, drinking, conversation . . . and the list goes on.

❀ Playing Columbo. No one likes to be questioned for hours about his or her past, as if a decision is about to be made immediately, based on this information.

❀ Forgetting to use your best manners: napkins go only on your lap—not tucked into your collar or belt; elbows off the table; do not start eating until the food has arrived for everyone at the table; and do not let your utensils touch the tablecloth once they've been used.

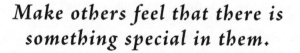

Make others feel that there is something special in them.

Tips a Lady Should Know

Being born a Rockefeller does not automatically give one class. Here are some basic tips a lady should know to put her well on her way to being a real lady.

❉ She should hold her drink with her left hand in order to shake hands and have her right hand free to socialize.

❉ A lady will never hesitate to wait for a gentleman to pull out her chair or open a door for her.

❉ She will face the people who are already in their seats when she makes her way down the row in a crowded theater. A lady never forces others to stare at her backside.

❉ She won't apply lipstick at the table—only in the powder room.

❉ If she must excuse herself from the dinner table, she simply says, "Excuse me." No further details are necessary.

❉ If she must bend over to pick up something, she always bends from the knees—and never sticks her behind in the air.

❉ She'll wear clothes that are not so revealing that they embarrass others, and if she is unsure how to dress for an occasion, she should ask her host.

❉ She will not put items on the dining table, such as sunglasses, a portfolio, or her cell phone. These items belong on the floor, beside her, or in her handbag.

❉ She should never hang her handbag over the back of her chair.

❋ She always sits with her back to the door of a restaurant, with the exception of wall seating, when her date sits in the chair facing the wall, and the lady sits against the wall, facing out.

❋ She may allow her date to order for her, but it is perfectly acceptable for her to order for herself.

Tips a Gentleman Should Know

Here are things every man should know if he wants to be a real gentleman and impress his date and others around him.

* He always opens doors for a lady.

* He will stand when being introduced and remain standing until the lady is seated.

* He never hesitates to pull out a chair for a lady.

* If he extends the invitation—he pays. (And in all cases, he *offers* to pay.)

* He should NEVER use a toothpick!

* He should always keep his eyes on his date; he will never allow his eyes to stray to other women or the television on the wall behind her head.

* He keeps his cell phone on silent and refrains from checking his PDA for e-mails and text messages until after he has taken his date safely home.

* He knows the **B.M.W.**s of dining (**B**read on left—**M**eal in center—**W**ater on right).

* His date always sits to his right.

* He remembers that "being a gentleman" overrules all other rules!

Homecoming and Coming Home Etiquette

꿀

Practice and prepare. Go on a practice date with a parent to brush up on your manners and to avoid major faux pas during the big night.

Tips

Homecoming:

❋ Do not fumble with your flowers. The corsage and boutonniere always go on the left. Don't hesitate to get help from one of your date's parents to avoid an awkward situation.

❋ Be extra polite. Do not forget your "yes, ma'ams," "no, sirs," "pleases," and "thank yous." Parents love this!

❋ Do not forget basic dining dos and don'ts. Remember **B.M.W.** (not the car): **B**read on the left, **M**eal in the middle, and **W**ater on the right.

❋ Never forget, ladies first in all things. Men always open doors and pull out chairs for their dates.

Tips

Coming Home:
(*Alumni*)

❋ Avoid awkward introductions. If you cannot remember a former classmate's name, introduce your spouse/date and give the classmate a chance to follow suit by introducing himself or herself.

❋   Be careful with your compliments. What you think may be a compliment ("You look great; you've lost a lot of weight!") could be misinterpreted and cause embarrassment for you both.

❋   Remember your home team colors. Be sure to dress appropriately for the game—it is a major faux pas to wear the other team's colors!

❋   Be yourself! No need to put on airs for people you have not seen in years.

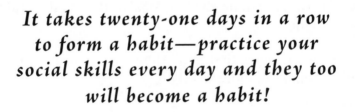

It takes twenty-one days in a row to form a habit—practice your social skills every day and they too will become a habit!

Breakup Etiquette

When a relationship ends, you need to handle the situation very delicately and be sensitive of the other person's feelings.

Tips

❀ Always break up in person. Breaking up over the phone is beyond tacky, and e-mail breakups are worse. Whatever you do, do not just drop off the radar screen never to be found again (not returning calls or showing up for dates). Relationships deserve face-to-face closure.

❀ Break up in an unromantic, low key, neutral place. Don't break up during the middle of dinner or on the way to a New Year's Eve party.

❀ Avoid rambling on about where the relationship went wrong and why breaking up is the best thing for both of you. Emotions can spin out of control fast. Saying, "You are a great person, but I just do not feel the same way about you," will sufficiently crush the person with whom you are breaking up.

❀ Do not be afraid to break up for fear of being alone. A "better than nothing" dating relationship is taking up time that could be spent finding the right person.

❀ Stick to your decision. Do not fall into the "second chance syndrome."

❀ Do not involve your mutual friends in the breakup. Avoid putting them in the awkward position of having to choose sides.

- Return all personal possessions such as books, CDs, or family heirlooms (grandmother's engagement ring); however, gifts should be kept. Make sure to distinguish between gifts and things borrowed that should be returned.
- Give each other necessary space to heal. Avoid calling the person for any reason, and skip going to the same places he or she will likely frequent.
- Remember, the heartbreak of a breakup takes time to heal. Do not immediately jump into another relationship to ease the pain. Take one day at a time and wait until you are emotionally ready to date again.
- Avoid making any big purchase decisions. This can lead to financial stress and is only a very quick (but temporary) fix for the heartbreak pain you are going through.

Wedding Etiquette

Avoid these situations when attending a wedding or reception. This is the biggest day in the lives of the bride and groom; please do not mess it up for them.

Faux Pas

* Being late! "Better late than never" does not apply at weddings. Walking in while the wedding ceremony is being held is an absolute embarrassment to everyone.

* Not sending in the RSVP card ASAP. It is crucial to send the response card immediately in order for the bride to plan the details of her wedding.

* Bringing babies or small children to a wedding. Crying babies and rambunctious children do not want to be at the event, nor do the bride and groom want them to destroy the romance of their wedding.

* Dressing in solid white. Any way you look at it—it is still a faux pas to dress in solid white, even if the bride is not in white. It still sends a signal that you are competing with the bride. It is her day in the spotlight and white is reserved for the bride, whether she chooses to wear it or not.

* Taking a gift to the wedding. Even though there will probably be a gift table at the wedding/reception, it is for the people who still do not understand that it is rude to bring a gift to the wedding. Send the gift to the couple ahead of time or after the wedding.

* Not respecting cultural differences. If you attend a wedding not of your own culture, you must respect their customs. Never be embarrassed to ask what is expected—it can be very helpful.

✱ Allowing your cell phone to ring. Turn your cell phone and pager off! It will be a disaster if your cell phone rings at the wedding, and for crying out loud, if it rings ... don't answer it!

✱ Making wrong acknowledgements. Telling the bride *"congratulations"* is like saying to her, "You finally found a husband!" It is appropriate to greet the bride with "best wishes" and the groom with "congratulations."

✱ Not sending thank-you notes for gifts. Believe it or not, there are people who do not take the time to send a thank-you note to those who send gifts to honor their marriage. It is unacceptable to overlook sending a thank-you note as soon as you receive the gift.

✱ Not sending the gift back to the giver if the wedding is canceled. Send a simple note stating that the wedding has been canceled, and along with the note, return any gifts you may have received. No explanation is necessary.

Tips for Wedding Party Etiquette

The bride and groom have waited their entire lives for this event. They have a support system in place to assist them in making sure their wedding is a complete success. Here are the major responsibilities of the wedding party.

❋ The **maid of honor** is responsible for helping the bride get dressed, adjusting her veil and train before she walks down the aisle, holding the groom's ring if there is no ring bearer, and making sure the other bridesmaids understand what is expected of them during the wedding.

❋ The **maid of honor** and **bridesmaids** are responsible for paying for their dresses, should be at the wedding rehearsal and rehearsal dinner, and should attend as many wedding showers as possible.

❋ The **wedding party** is not required to buy a gift for every party they are asked to attend. They are there to support and assist the bride and groom in any way possible.

❋ The **best man** is responsible for ensuring that the groom gets to the ceremony on time and is also responsible for ensuring that the bride's rings are available if there is no ring bearer.

❋ The **best man** is also responsible for making sure that all of the groom's attendants have their marching orders—measuring, picking up, and paying for their own formal wear, and being at the church on time.

❀ The **best man** is responsible for giving the first toast at the wedding rehearsal and the wedding reception, followed by the father of the bride, and then the father of the groom.

❀ The **mother of the bride** is responsible for contacting the mother of the groom to discuss the attire the mothers will be wearing at the wedding. The bride's mother chooses her dress first, and the groom's mother chooses her dress to coordinate. Typically, for a formal wedding, the mothers will wear a long or tea-length dress.

❀ The **groom's parents** typically pay for the rehearsal dinner and the bride's parents pay for the wedding (except for the groom's cake—the groom or his family pays).

❀ **Flower girls** and **ring bearers** are typically between four and eight years old. It is best to ask the children if they want to be in the wedding instead of forcing them to be in it. It is also important to explain the event and the expectation you will have of the children prior to the wedding. Some little girls think they are getting married and some ring bearers think it is their job to clean up after the flower girl drops the petals.

❀ There is typically one **usher** for every fifty guests. It is the usher's responsibility to make sure the guests sit on either the bride's or groom's side of the aisle, depending on with whom the guests have the closer relationship.

$$\sim\!\curlyvee\!\sim$$

Wedding Ring Etiquette

Many times a widow may ask what is proper concerning wearing her wedding ring after her husband's death.

There is no official rule, so do what makes you most comfortable. Some widows wear their rings on their right hand; others remove their rings, saving them for future generations. Some have their rings fashioned into a special piece of jewelry, and others choose to keep wearing their rings on their left hand for the rest of their lives. As you can see, it is strictly up to you to do what makes you feel most comfortable.

Anniversary Etiquette

I receive countless questions regarding anniversary celebrations. I will incorporate the most frequently asked questions and the answers in the tips below.

Tips

* You are responsible for paying for the party if you planned it. If someone asks you about the expense and wants to chip in, that is a bonus for you. In other words, do not come up with a great idea to throw your parents a fiftieth wedding anniversary celebration and expect the other siblings or relatives to help pay for the event.

* We all know cost can be a factor. Before planning the anniversary party, it is appropriate to let the other siblings or close family members involved know about your plans and let each decide if they want to donate to the expense.

* It is not appropriate to request money as a gift for the couple. If someone *asks* you if the couple would appreciate money as a gift, you can say, "Yes, thank you!"

* Allow the most qualified person to plan the celebration. There is no set rule as to who should plan the anniversary celebration—it should not necessarily be the oldest child, nor the one with the most money, nor the one relative who lives closest. The person who is the best party planner should be the one who takes on the planning responsibility.

❋ It is perfectly acceptable for the couple celebrating the anniversary to plan their own party. They do not have to wait on a family member or close friend to throw a party in their honor.

❋ The celebrated couple should feel comfortable in giving a short speech—either thanking the people who gave them the party, or if they gave their own party, thanking the people who attended.

❋ Guests do not have to bring a gift to the celebration, but it is never wrong to bring one—unless the invitation requests "no gifts, please." (At least take a beautiful anniversary card.)

❋ Always attach a note card with your name to your gift. What a shame for the couple to unwrap the gift you picked out for them and never know who brought it.

❋ You are not expected to bring a gift that represents the year of the anniversary (example: fifty-year anniversary gift is gold). A well-thought-out gift is the best kind, not relative to the expense. Take a gift that will be special to the couple.

❋ Remember, you should always send thank-you notes for the gifts received and to those who gave the celebration for you.

Excellent timeless anniversary gift ideas include beautiful photo albums, bookends, or picture frames.

Part Four

Christmas and Party Etiquette

The Christmas season is the busiest time of the year. We go more places, buy more gifts, and attend more parties during this time than any other season of the year. This can be a very stressful time if we do not know how to give a party or what is expected of us as we attend parties. The information in the following chapters will add fun back into your holiday season.

❋ Top Ten Christmas Holiday Faux Pas

❋ Etiquette Tips for Christmas

❋ Christmas Office Gift-Giving Etiquette

❋ Children's Holiday Etiquette

❋ Host and Hostess Etiquette

Top Ten Christmas Holiday Faux Pas

Over 50 percent of our socializing occurs during the holiday season. To enhance your enjoyment of this special time, avoid these top ten most common faux pas people commit during this season.

1. Making excuses when someone surprises you with a gift. People make the situation worse when they make excuses or go overboard with apologies because they do not have a gift to exchange. Just say "thank you" and follow up with a thank-you note. You can always send a gift later.

2. Married couples signing their Christmas cards with the husband's name first. The husband's first name should not be separated from his last name. Many people think the husband's name should go first as in "Chuck and Robin Corbin," but the correct way for married couples to write their name is "Robin and Chuck Corbin."

3. Sneezing into your social hand. Your right hand is your social hand. No one wants to reach out and shake hands with someone who has just sneezed into this hand.

4. Asking someone why he or she is not drinking alcohol. There are many reasons people say no to cocktails and often they are personal. There is no reason to put someone on the spot.

5. Waiting until the last minute to respond to a party invitation. This gives an impression that you are holding out for something better to come up and makes it more difficult for the hostess to make plans for the party.

6. Forgetting to attach a card to a hostess gift. Always take a hostess gift to a party with an attached card that has your name on it so the hostess will know who brought the gift.

7. Double dipping. Not only is it gross, but it can be a health hazard to dunk food into a dip after you have taken a bite of the food.

8. Not standing when being introduced. Whenever possible, it is respectful to stand when being introduced—men and women.

9. Leaving a party and telling the hosts you have to go to another party. Thank the hosts for inviting you and for a wonderful party. If you must, just tell them you do have another commitment. Do not tell them you are going to the Joneses' blowout Christmas party, and you cannot wait to get there.

10. Thinking everyone loves your pet as much as you do. Many people are allergic to pets and do not want them hanging around during a holiday party.

Etiquette Tips for Christmas

The following top ten tips are basic but easy to overlook. Take a minute to review this list, as it will help you both personally and professionally during the holiday season.

1. Always err on the side of being conservative, especially when it comes to:

    a. Drinking

    b. Dressing

    c. Gift-giving

    Being excessive and extreme with any of these can cause you much embarrassment.

2. You must attend your company Christmas party. This is a "must attend" event and can be a career-killer if you decide not to go—this shows disrespect for your company, supervisors, and colleagues.

3. Thank the host/hostess for the party by:

    a. Bringing a gift to the host/hostess to show your appreciation.

    b. Thanking the host/hostess before you leave the party.

    c. Sending a thank-you note afterwards.

4. Give gifts that honor the recipients. Know their taste and always give a well-thought-out gift.

5. When uncertain, call to confirm the proper "holiday attire." This term can have various meanings to different people. It could mean anything from a sweater to holiday sequins.

6. RSVP/ASAP—Always respond within a few days of receiving an invitation. The host/hostess needs to know how many people will attend in order to plan the party.

7. Please keep your cell phone on manner mode at holiday parties. It is not impressive to "cell yell" over the crowd. If you must talk on your phone—go somewhere private.

8. Maintain a balanced conversation. Refrain from boring "business talk" or too much "kid talk."

9. Prioritize socializing at holiday parties, instead of just eating and drinking.

10. Attempt to send a thank-you note for gifts within the first week if possible. However, thank-you notes are always better late than never!

Treat others the way you want to be treated.

Christmas Office Gift-Giving Etiquette

Gift giving at the office can be confusing. The following tips will set you up for success as you make your gift-giving decisions.

Tips

※ Always err on the side of being conservative—especially when it comes to gift giving. Being excessive or extreme can cause you and the other person to be uncomfortable. Be aware of cultural, religious, or international taboos. If the gift is for an individual, try to tailor it to the individual's hobbies or interests. Make certain the gift cannot, in any way, be misconstrued as "too personal," especially across gender lines.

※ Avoid giving alcohol unless you know the recipient on a close, personal basis. Many people do not drink alcohol for religious and/or personal reasons.

※ Always send a thank-you note immediately after receiving a gift.

※ You may choose to send your gift as a Thanksgiving or New Year's gift—this will make it stand out from the rest.

※ Check the corporate policy. Contact the personnel department of a company for their gift-giving guidelines.

※ Be sure to include an enclosure card, hand signed by you, preferably with a meaningful message that relates to the gift and the recipient.

❀ Make a sincere effort to present the gift in person. Personally handing a gift to someone has a much greater impact than if a delivery person leaves it with a receptionist or at the person's desk.

❀ Wrap the gift. Presentation is everything!

Supervisors:

❀ Be consistent from year to year when giving gifts to employees. If you gave a lavish gift last year and are now cutting back because of budgetary concerns, communicate that to your employees. You do not want them thinking their work was not appreciated.

❀ Definitely buy your direct assistant a gift. A bonus does not count as a gift. Make sure it is not too personal.

❀ Give gifts intended for selected individuals in a discreet manner so as not to offend those who did not receive a gift.

Clients/Vendors:

❀ Reconsider giving a gift if you have any concerns about the appropriateness of this gesture, or how it might be construed. Always guard against even the appearance of impropriety. It can only hurt a business relationship . . . it will never help.

Children's Holiday Etiquette

ᴄᎾ

Train up a child in the way he should go, and when he is old, he will not depart from it. (Proverbs 22:6)

Tips

❈ We all know that every parent fears that his or her children will voice a dreadful comment in front of the giver of a holiday gift and will embarrass everyone. Parents must help children practice being gracious when receiving gifts and remembering that it is the thought that counts.

❈ Always write thank-you notes immediately after receiving a gift and after going to a party. This is a fundamental practice that should be taught to children as soon as they are old enough to write.

❈ It is a certainty that your children will attend many parties and meet new people during the holiday season. Teach them to always stand when being introduced, look the person in the eye, give a firm handshake, and be gracious.

❈ Our table manners are important. Families will spend much time around the table during the holidays. Remember that basic table manners will speak volumes about your children's social skills. For example, children should know which bread plate and water glass is theirs, and should remember **B.M.W.**: **B**read (left), **M**eal (middle), **W**ater (right). Also, no elbows on the table; hold your utensils like pencils, not like handlebars; and butter your roll one bite at a time—do not eat it like an apple.

❈ No double dipping, please!

❃ Do not forget that "please" and "thank you" are phrases that should be used over and over again during the holidays. Practice saying them sincerely.

❃ Teach children about the basics of party behavior during the holidays. For example, they should know about responding to a holiday party invitation immediately, taking a small hostess gift, and writing a thank-you note afterwards.

❃ Encourage your children to be sensitive to other children who do not celebrate the Christmas holidays.

❃ Always adhere to the gift price limit that is established for parties your children will be attending so as not to make others feel deprived—and remind your child never to talk about the expense of the gift he or she may give.

❃ Encourage the older kids to be sensitive to younger children and the truths of Santa Claus.

❃ Teach your children to remember their guest manners when they go to someone's house for a holiday occasion: no running or horseplay in the house, eat only in designated areas, do not touch decorations or decorative items on display, do not go into rooms unless invited to do so, and always use their "manners voice" when in others' homes.

Host and Hostess Etiquette

Be the perfect host and hostess when you have over-night guests.

Tips

* Before guests arrive, set expectations on details such as length of stay, daily routine, pets, smoking, parking, etc.

* Always have the guest room clean and ready when your guests arrive.

* Let your guest know when meals will be served, and provide details on any meals that will be eaten out.

* Show your guest around your home and be sure to include information and locations on snacks and drinks, extra blankets and towels, and all electronics including intrusion alarms, computer hookups, and remote controls.

* Find out what your guests would like to do while visiting, and plan activities with their input.

* Make sure your guests have a key or access to your home so they can come and go as they wish if they are going to be with you for an extended stay.

* Discuss transportation needs with your guests, and provide a map of the city with points of interest shown.

* Make sure your guests have privacy and time to themselves.

* Most importantly—make your guests feel at home. Remember to treat them the way you would want to be treated.

Houseguest Etiquette

Be the perfect houseguest—maybe you will be invited again.

Tips

❋ Always bring a well-thought-out gift and present it upon arrival to show your appreciation. Such thoughtfulness makes a great first impression!

❋ Do not eat, drink, or use anything without asking first.

❋ Find out immediately where your host wants you to park your vehicle during the daytime and overnight.

❋ Ask before you bring a guest or pet with you. Your host may not love Fi-Fi or Benji as much as you do!

❋ Refrain from smoking in someone else's home. Always ask for an acceptable place you can smoke.

❋ Do not expect to be waited on or served. Always offer to help with the household duties. For example, be sure to make your bed each day, keep the bathroom and other areas you use clean, and ask what to do with used towels and laundry.

❋ Offer to buy groceries and/or pay for an evening out when you have an extended stay (more than three days).

❋ Always (always!) send a thank-you note immediately after your visit.

❋ Do not overstay your welcome. If you have the feeling it's time to go, it probably is!

Part Five

Handling Bad News, Including Funerals

Many times we are faced with bad news or difficult situations and quite simply do not know how to respond. In many situations, our first reaction is not always the right one. These chapters will offer valuable advice on handling bad news, and planning and attending a funeral.

❋ Things Not to Say

❋ More Things Not to Say

❋ Funeral Attendee Etiquette

❋ Funeral Tips for the Family of the Deceased

Things Not to Say When a Friend . . .

Oftentimes when we are presented with startling news, we say the first thing that comes to our mind, and many times, it is inappropriate. Here are some examples of situations in which a friend . . .

. . . *tells you he has lost his job.*

Do not say:

❀ "OH, NO! What in the world are you going to do?"

❀ "I hope you gave them a piece of your mind before you left!"

❀ "That was not a good place to work anyway."

Better to say:

❀ "You are very talented—you are going to do great. Let me know how I can help you during this transition."

. . . *tells you that a family member died.*

Do not say:

❀ "He lived a long life."

❀ "She's in a better place now."

❀ "What are you going to do with the home and belongings?"

Better to say:

❀ "I am so sorry for your loss. Please know that I am here for you in any way you need me. You and your family are in my thoughts and prayers."

... confides he is in serious debt.

Do not say:

❀ "How much in debt are you?"

❀ "What in the world did you spend that much money on?"

❀ "I hope this teaches you a lesson in money management."

Better to say:

❀ "This happens to many people and you will pull out of it—it will take patience, time, and maybe even a financial advisor."

... announces she is getting a divorce.

Do not say:

❀ "Finally! It's about time. He was no good anyway—you can do better!"

❀ "Do you mind if I go out with him?"

❀ "Is there someone else—did you catch him cheating on you?"

Better to say:

❀ "As a friend, I want to make sure you have considered all options, including reconciliation. I am here for you—please let me know what I can do to help."

… *tells you his kids have messed up.*

Do not say:

* ❃ "Well, here is what I think you should do with them …"

* ❃ "What did you expect—it was only a matter of time!"

* ❃ "You had better get control over those kids before they do something really bad!"

Better to say:

* ❃ "We have all made mistakes; hopefully the children will learn from them. Let me know if I can be of any assistance in this difficult situation."

… *confesses she cheated on her spouse.*

Do not say:

* ❃ "That is the dumbest thing you could have ever done, and I do not want to be your friend anymore!"

* ❃ "I am going to tell your spouse—what you are doing is wrong!"

* ❃ "Be careful, and don't get caught."

Better to say:

* ❃ "I care about you and want the best for you, but have you considered all the consequences of your actions?"

... *tells you she has been diagnosed with a serious illness.*

Do not say:

❋ "I knew someone who had this illness, and she successfully fought it for six years before she died."

❋ "Are you sure you've got a good doctor?"

❋ "You will be fine—do not even worry about it!"

Better to say:

❋ "Please let me know if there is anything I can do to help you at any time. I am here for you. I will keep you in my prayers."

More Things Not to Say When a Friend ...

۵Ĵى

... *tells you she had a miscarriage.*

Do not say:

* "It was not meant to be."

* "You will have other children."

* "Your baby is in Heaven and is one of God's little angels."

Better to say:

* "I am so sorry for your loss. Please know that I am here for you in any way you need me. You and your family are in my thoughts and prayers."

... *smells to high heaven.*

Do not say:

* "What is that awful smell?"

* "Wow, someone really has bad B.O."

* "Did you forget your deodorant this morning?"

Better to say:

* "I need to discuss a subject that is difficult for me to talk about, but I would want you to bring it up in private with me if it were the other way around. That is why I am telling you, as a friend, that your body odor is an issue." (You can then offer suggestions for dealing with the issue, if necessary—bath, deodorant, or maybe medical assistance.)

... tells you the unusual name of her baby.

Do not say:

❀ "You are kidding me."

❀ "That must be a family name—what are you going to really call her?"

❀ "Boy, are the kids going to really tease her when she gets older."

Better to say:

❀ "What a wonderful and unique name."

... shows up in the same dress.

Do not say:

❀ "How embarrassing; I am going home!"

❀ "Do you mind if we stay away from each other during this party?"

❀ Continually saying to others: "Suzy and I have on the same dress!"

Better to:

❀ First of all, do not mention it to others, because most people will not notice unless you bring it up. However, you can say, "Love what you have on! We have great taste," or even say, "Great minds think alike." Then, do not bring it up again!

... has no respect for cell phone or PDA manners.

Do not say:

* ❁ "Who in the world are you talking to?"

* ❁ "Do you think you are so important that you can be disrespectful to others by yelling on your cell phone in public?"

* ❁ Nothing, but give her dirty looks and shake your head.

Better to say:

* ❁ "Before we go into this public place, I'm putting my cell phone on silent; what about you?"

* ❁ If she gets into a loud conversation on the phone, motion for her to step outside to finish her conversation or to lower her voice. Let her know later that you are sure she was unaware of how loud her voice was when she was on the cell phone.

... eats off your bread plate or takes your drink.

Do not say:

* ❁ "Excuse me—that plate was mine!"

* ❁ "Can you please hand me your bread plate?"

* ❁ "Let me teach you some etiquette tips."

Better to say:

* ❁ In private: "Excuse me, waiter, may I have another bread plate (or drink)?"

... tells a controversial joke.

Do not say:

❉   "I can top that one!"

❉   Nothing at all while standing there listening and then laughing.

❉   Verbally rip him apart in front of everyone.

Better to say:

❉   Walking away from the conversation speaks volumes; or gently say: "I know you do not realize it, but it is inappropriate to tell this kind of joke."

... lets his pet run wild.

Do not say:

❉   "Your pet runs wild, just like your children."

❉   "If that cat comes near me again, I am going to kick it into its next life!"

❉   "How do you live like this?"

Better to say:

❉   "Fi-Fi is an adorable dog, but may I ask a big favor? Please put him in another room." (Then, if possible, give the reason, such as allergies or fear of dogs.)

... is double-dipping.

Do not say:

❈ Nothing at all.

❈ "That's gross! You just contaminated the entire dip with your germs."

Better to say:

❈ Tell the host of the party to handle the situation. If all else fails, gently say, "I know you do not realize it, but you are double-dipping."

... has spinach in her teeth.

Do not say:

❈ Whisper about it behind her back with someone else.

❈ Ask if she enjoyed the spinach she had for lunch.

❈ Tell her about it in front of a group of people.

Better to say:

❈ In private: "I would want you to tell me, so I wanted you to know that you have spinach stuck in your teeth. Just thought you might want to excuse yourself and take care of it."

Funeral Attendee Etiquette

The loss of a family member or friend is a very difficult situation for all involved. We should do our part to express our sympathy and support the family any way we can. These tips will help you be more considerate.

Tips

* Call or visit the family. The moment you learn of the death of a friend or relative, call and/or visit the home of the family to offer sympathy and support.

* Ask what you can do to help. Help is always greatly appreciated when there is a death in the family. Bringing a meal for the family, helping to make phone calls, or assisting with child care will be appreciated.

* Send a sympathy card. It is appropriate to send a sympathy card even if you are only an acquaintance. It's best sent as soon as you learn of the death, but there is no time limit on sending sympathy cards.

* Do not hesitate to ask. Ask if the family prefers donations or flowers, ask about religious practices that are different from your own, and ask for other ways you can pay your respects to the family.

* Make a donation. If the funeral notice says, "in lieu of flowers," everyone who would like to send a remembrance should follow the request.

* Keep your condolence simple. Simple statements such as, "I'm sorry for your loss," "My sympathy to you and your family," or "John was a fine person and he will be missed," are best.

❀ Attend the visitation. Visitation is an opportunity for people to pay their respects prior to the funeral. Visitations may be held in the home of the deceased or the funeral home. Most people will only stay at the visitation about fifteen minutes, but use your judgment—close friends and family should plan to stay longer if the bereaved family needs support.

❀ Decide what to wear. Funerals are still a time to dress in subtle colors (unless the family is having a celebration of life and has requested that you wear bright colors).

❀ Briefly pass by the open casket to pay your respects, but you do not have to participate if this is uncomfortable for you.

❀ Do not take a seat in the first few rows at the service—these seats are reserved for the family of the deceased.

❀ Follow up with the bereaved. Mourning can take a long time. Friends should be especially sensitive to the widow/widower on special occasions such as anniversaries and birthdays.

Funeral Tips for the Family of the Deceased

A true friend is one who is there with you in times of need. There may be no greater need than when you lose a loved one and face the difficult task of planning the funeral. In times like these, do not hesitate to call on your friends for help—they want to be there for you.

❋ Ask for help. Friends and family want to do something to help and this is a time you need to rely on others. People will ask, "What can I do to help?" and you should tell them—and be specific: "I need calls made," or "I need these movies returned," or "I need someone to go with me to pick out a dress for the funeral."

❋ Delegate tasks. Appoint one person to be in charge of flowers. He or she should collect cards that come with the flowers and write a description of the flowers on the outside of each envelope. This will be a tremendous help when writing thank-you notes.

❋ Do not go alone to the funeral home to make the final plans. Ask a trusted friend or clergy member who has been through the process to attend funeral home meetings with you. You will need to make decisions about the funeral, and it is best to have someone who can help you make sound decisions. This is a very stressful time for you, and it is always good to seek the advice of others, especially someone who has shared this same experience.

❊ Be honest with children. Use realistic, age-appropriate terms, and do not explain death by saying, "Grandpa is asleep," or other phrases that could confuse children. Children will ask the questions they want and need to know. Give them an honest answer, or seek help from a clergy member, therapist, or trusted friend on ways to talk to children about death.

❊ Select funeral attendants. Ask male family members, friends, and business or spiritual associates to serve as pallbearers and ushers during the funeral.

❊ Keep comments brief. In reply to visitors' comments, simply say, "Thank you for coming," or "John spoke of you often," or "You're very kind." You are not obligated to engage in lengthy conversations.

❊ Give an honorarium. It is appropriate for the family of the deceased to make a financial gift or "honorarium" to the clergy member presiding over the funeral. A typical honorarium for a clergy person is at least one hundred dollars.

❊ Share the costs. Immediate family should share in the cost of the funeral if prior arrangements have not been made.

❊ Ask someone to stay at your home during the funeral. This is an awful fact of life, but some pathetic people read the obituary columns to find out when funerals are being held, and then they rob the house. Believe it or not, this is a very common occurrence.

❊ Acknowledge gifts and assistance. Write short notes to acknowledge gifts of flowers, donations, food, or other assistance people give you. Notes should be written within a month of the funeral if at all possible, but people will understand if notes arrive later.

* Give yourself permission to grieve. You will be very busy planning the funeral and staying in task mode, which might keep you from grieving deeply, but realize you may collapse after the funeral, so give yourself permission to mourn.

Part Six

Decisions, Decisions, Decisions...

Situations We Face on a Daily Basis

Every day we face many situations and frankly, we do not know how to handle them, so we just stumble through and do the best we can. Here are ways to handle some of the more common dilemmas.

* Dinner Party Etiquette

* Top Ten Toasting Etiquette Tips

* Limousine and Town Car Etiquette

* Movie Theater Etiquette

* Golf Etiquette

* Driving Etiquette

* Petiquette

* Pregnancy Etiquette

* Gym Etiquette

Dinner Party Etiquette

Our friend Susanne Forbes Dicker gives the most extravagant dinner parties and is a magnificent hostess. Whether she invites us to her home or a private dining room of a fine restaurant, one secret I have found is that she makes each party warm and personal for every guest—and the food is always delicious. Just in case you are invited to her home for dinner, or if you decide to have a dinner party of your own, you will benefit from the tips below. Enjoy!

Tips

For the invited guest:

* BE ON TIME! It is a huge faux pas to be late for a sit-down dinner party; however, if you have an emergency, call immediately to let the host/hostess know you will be late.

* As soon as you receive the invitation, let the host/hostess know if you are allergic to any foods, pets, or scents.

* Bring a host/hostess gift. (Do not bring flowers unless they are in a vase.) This is a small token of appreciation for the time and effort of hosting the party.

* Everyone—turn your cell phone on manner mode. (Must I say this again? . . . *Yes, I must!*)

* Never bring a guest with you without getting prior approval from your host/hostess.

* Do not start to eat until everyone has been served and your host or hostess picks up his or her first utensil.

❋ Do not dominate the conversation(s) at the dining table. Allow others to talk, too! Make it a point to talk to the person on each side of you for the same amount of time.

❋ Compliment the host/hostess on the food. (Don't go overboard—your compliments will sound insincere!)

❋ Pace yourself—never eat faster or slower than everyone else.

❋ Never eat and run; stay to visit after the meal.

❋ Remember, if you must drink—know your limit on alcohol and do not go over it.

❋ Write a thank-you note to the hostess immediately afterwards.

For the host/hostess:

❋ Invite each person at least two weeks in advance—that is, if you want to be considered a good host and hostess.

❋ Meet each guest at the door—the welcome sets the tone for the entire night.

❋ Make proper introductions.

❋ Sit on each end of the table, or across from each other at a round table.

❋ Instruct the guest of honor (should you have one) to sit to your right.

❋ Take into consideration each guest's personality so the conversations will flow. In other words, do not seat two introverts side by side, and you should not put two drama queens together.

❊ Also, remember to seat your guests male/female and to seat couples apart.

❊ Place cards are appropriate so your guest knows where to sit, or you may choose to verbally tell each guest his or her designated seat.

❊ The host/hostess is not required to open gifts in the presence of company. (Also, one is not required to send a thank-you note for this gift!)

❊ *FYI*—You will not be a candidate for "Socialite of the Year" if you have a BYOB dinner party or a potluck dinner party!

(Also please refer to page 28 for dining tips and faux pas before attending the next dinner party.)

ᷤᵧ

> *We are all like diamonds; we all have a basic value but it is not until we are polished that our true worth is recognized.*

Top Ten Toasting Etiquette Tips

There are three B's to remember when it comes to toasting: **Begin, Be Brief, and Be Seated!** Here are some other tips that will make you more comfortable when participating in a toast.

1. You may give a toast at the beginning of the dinner or event, or at the beginning of the dessert course. The best toast is one minute or less in length.

2. The host is the first to give a toast to the guest or guests of honor.

3. The host should stand if there is a possibility that everyone can't hear the toast, and then raise his glass halfway while looking at the guest of honor as he gives the toast.

4. Other guests may then propose a toast, following the host.

5. The guest of honor should reciprocate with a toast before dessert.

6. You should never "drink to yourself"—it is the same as congratulating yourself! If the toast is offered in your honor, do not pick up your glass. This will prevent you from being tempted to take a drink when everyone else drinks to you.

7. It is not necessary to clank glasses together and shout "cheers" when toasting.

8. Never refuse to participate in a toast. You do not have to drink alcohol to participate in a toast, nor do you have to drink from a champagne flute—fill your glass with your drink of choice.

9. Do not use a utensil to tap on the side of the glass to get everyone's attention. This will many times result in a crack in the crystal.

10. If you are making a toast in a roomful of people, not at dinner, move to a platform or the center of the room so everyone can hear the toast.

Limousine or Town Car Etiquette

A limousine or town car is an easy and efficient mode of transportation. Some might need a driver in order to do business while en route, and some might rent a driver so they look like a rock star. Whatever the case, I am all for it! Everyone should have a personal chauffeur if it can be afforded. Here are tips to assist you in "the road well traveled!"

Tips

❋ Request a car that is for non-smokers—unless, of course, you are a smoker.

❋ Make sure to find out the color, make, and model of the limo. Believe me, they might send a car that looks like it is pre-owned by Uncle Fester and the Addams Family.

❋ Determine how many people will be riding, and find out the cost of a sedan versus a limousine. A stretch can cost four times the amount of a town car.

❋ Allow the chauffeur or driver to open the door for you. Do not be tempted to open the door and get in or out on your own.

❋ Remember, the power seat in the limo is the curbside seat or the back right seat.

❋ Be aware that the jump seat (the seat facing backward) is the junior executive seat, and is also considered the most uncomfortable seat.

❋ The back middle seat is the next most uncomfortable seat in the car. Do not allow the key person in your group to get stuck in this seat or the jump seat.

❀ Make sure that when you take a seat in the limo (or any vehicle), sit down in the seat first, swing your legs in, and slide over if necessary. Do not step in first, causing your backside (rear end) to stick up in the air.

❀ Add 20 percent gratuity (for good service, of course!) for the driver, but always make sure the tip has not been added into the price automatically.

❀ Refrain from requesting that the driver exceed the speed limit or do anything else illegal.

Movie Theater Etiquette

Everyone will enjoy the movie even more if we all refrain from these common faux pas and follow the tips that accompany them. Enjoy the movie and allow others around you to do the same.

Faux Pas

❋ Wearing a cowboy hat inside the movie theater. Were you raised in a barn? Remember to take your hat off inside buildings.

❋ Forgetting to turn your cell phone on manner mode, or even worse, answering it. Remember that socializing with your friends on the phone during the movie is very distracting.

❋ Talking to the movie screen. It is a movie—the actors cannot hear you!

❋ Crying babies, noisy children, and ice crunchers are all major annoyances. Allow those around you the opportunity to enjoy the movie.

❋ Commandeering additional seats with your purse, handbags and/or coats is very inconsiderate. Take only the number of seats you need for your group.

❋ Coming and going during the movie. Get settled before the movie starts—leave only if you have an emergency.

❋ Walking through the aisle of seats facing the screen, forcing people to look at your backside. Walk down the aisle facing the people and be prepared to say, "Excuse me, please."

❋ Trashing the place. Put your empty containers, napkins, and wrappers in the litter receptacle on your way out.

❋ Arriving late! Be considerate of others and get settled with your drinks and snacks before the movie starts.

Golf Etiquette

Many play golf only on vacation or business trips and do not know the basic etiquette to follow. Observing these rules will enhance your enjoyment of the game (and the enjoyment had by others on the course).

Tips

* Take several lessons before playing so you can at least hit the ball and keep it moving forward. The homeowners near the golf course will appreciate you more if your ball doesn't fly through their picture window.

* Allow groups behind you to pass if you are playing slowly and if there is an open hole in front of you. This is a game, not a career.

* Dress appropriately—most courses require collared shirts.

* Remember, the person with the lowest score on the previous hole hits first on the next hole, and the person with the highest score goes last. However, most courses play "ready golf." Whoever is ready on the tee box should step up and tee off—it speeds up play.

* Realize that golf is a game of integrity—you keep your own score and tell others if you violated a rule that affects your score.

* Do not allow two golfers to play with one set of clubs—it slows down play and is not allowed on most courses.

* Never drive the golf cart on or near the putting greens. Normally the courses are marked to note restricted areas for the carts.

❁ Know that "Cart Path Only" means you cannot drive on the course at all, while the "Ninety Degree Rule" means you can leave the cart path when you are ninety degrees (straight across) from your ball.

❁ Do not talk or make noise when someone is preparing to hit the ball. This is one of the worst things you can do on the course—be quiet and be still when others are addressing the ball.

❁ Never walk between someone's ball and the hole when you are on the putting green—always walk around his or her ball.

❁ Always know the brand of ball you are hitting, and make sure you do not play someone else's ball.

❁ Do not panic and forget to yell "fore" if you hit your ball in the direction of other players.

❁ Always tip the bag person three to five dollars if he helps with your bags—depending upon his service, of course.

Driving Etiquette

Here's a list of driving tips—these may sound obvious, but I bet you could add a few more of your own pet peeves to this list.

Tips

❋ Park in a handicap parking space only if you are handicapped or have a handicapped person getting out of your vehicle.

❋ Please understand that multitasking (including reading, talking on a cell phone, and putting on mascara) is unacceptable and dangerous.

❋ Use your signals (we can't read your mind).

❋ Do not be the cause of an accident—slower drivers (Granny) should get in the right lane! The farther to the left, the faster the lane.

❋ Do not take two parking spaces, even if you do have a shiny new car.

❋ Turn it down, for crying out loud. Extremely loud music is cool (not!), but perhaps not too cool if it is shaking your car and the vehicles on both sides of you at the red light.

❋ Please be courteous and hold up a hand and wave if drivers are kind enough to slow down and let you in front of them in their lane.

❋ DO NOT speed up if you see a driver trying to turn into your lane. This is the number one cause of road rage!

❋ Stop tailgating … and stop it now! (If for no other reason—*it is illegal!!*)

Petiquette

Are you a dog lover or a cat fanatic? I will remain silent on my preference but cannot remain silent on the tips below that can make all of us better pet owners and neighbors.

Tips

❋ Do not allow your yapping dog to disturb the neighbors.

❋ Do not think it is cute if your dog takes a quick dip in the neighbor's swimming pool to cool off.

❋ Train your dog not to jump on guests; better yet, he should stay in another part of the house or even outside when you have company.

❋ Do not be persuaded by those cute puppy eyes—do not allow him to beg guests for food.

❋ Obey leash laws, and do not allow Spanky to run loose.

❋ While on a leash walk, never allow your dog to approach another dog without permission from the pet's owner.

❋ ALWAYS scoop the poop if Fido potties on someone else's yard, in a flowerbed, or on public property.

❋ Have your pet spayed or neutered so as not to add to the pet overpopulation crisis.

❋ Do not allow your kitty to climb on the neighbor's car (even the sneakiest of cats leaves paw prints).

❋ Keep your pet by your side and under control when at the veterinarian's office.

Pregnancy Etiquette

In trying to share in the excitement of hearing of a close friend or family member's pregnancy, we often say the wrong things. Heed this advice and keep a friend.

Tips

❋ Avoid comments about an expectant mother's weight and stories of difficult births.

❋ Always look the mom-to-be in the eye—not her belly—when talking to her, and avoid asking her every day: "How are you feeling?"

❋ Never hesitate to give an expectant mother a compliment or your chair—she can use both!

❋ Avoid the "tummy pat"—the impulse to touch an expectant mother's stomach.

❋ Avoid asking private questions such as, "Is your insurance paying for everything?" or "Are you coming back to work?"

❋ Treat a miscarriage like a death. Do not disregard it, offer advice, or say something as insensitive as, "I'm sure you'll have another." Instead, simply say, "I'm praying and thinking of you. I'm sorry to hear about your loss."

❋ Avoid giving advice on the baby's name. The name the parents have picked out might not be your favorite, but is a very special name to them.

✽ Avoid getting too personal. Questions about the baby's gender and doctor's visits can be too personal. Take the lead from the expectant mother, and only discuss the topics she addresses.

✽ Be certain before you ask, "When are you due?" This is a question that can be an embarrassment for life. You never can be sure if a woman is pregnant, or if she, perhaps, has already delivered her baby.

✽ Please consider that if you are planning a family, you should avoid saying, "We're trying to get pregnant!" This conjures up pictures that are too personal. Instead, say, "We hope to have children some day."

Gym Etiquette

Avoid the following mistakes while in the gym, and workouts will be better for everyone.

Faux Pas

* Monopolizing the equipment. Be mindful of people waiting to use the equipment you are using. Do not use more than one piece of equipment at a time, and do not sit on the weight machine between sets if others are waiting to use it. Also, limit length of time on cardio equipment if there are people waiting.

* Leaving weights on equipment. Be sure to put your weights up after you use a machine, and put away all equipment you used in a class (steps, bands, weights, or towels, for example).

* Saving equipment for others. Reserving equipment (such as treadmills or bikes in spin class) for friends is a definite faux pas! First come, first served!

* Going the wrong way or in the wrong lane on the track. Walkers should take the inside lane and runners should stay to the outside. Always pay attention to direction signs on the track, or if no signs are posted, go in the same direction as the rest of the people on the track.

* Doing the "cell yell" while working out. No matter where you are—restaurant, bus, or gym—talking loudly into your cell phone is rude and disturbing to people around you.

* Going to the gym when you are sick. Ewww! There is no need to spread germs, especially in a place where people are trying to get healthy!

❀ Not cleaning up after yourself. Towel off equipment before you leave, wipe up puddles you leave by the shower, toss disposable razors, and clean up any mess you make on the counters.

❀ Changing the channel. How rude to assume you are the only one watching the TV. Someone could be involved in a show. Always check with others first if you want to change the television channel.

❀ Hovering while someone is exercising. Don't stand and stare at someone while you are waiting to use equipment he or she is using—just be patient.

❀ Using gym towels as Kleenex. Another big Ewwww! This should not have to be mentioned, but unfortunately, it must: tissues are for noses, towels are for bodies. Do not confuse the two.

Part Seven

Growing Up...
for Young Children and Young Adults

In a world where rudeness runs rampant, parents have the responsibility to raise children as well-mannered adults, ones who are properly prepared for their places in society. One of the most frequently asked questions I receive from parents is, "At what age should I start teaching my children manners?" The answer is: from the time they are born ... and never stop! You should never let up or give up. Your children will grow up more confidently in every phase of childhood and adulthood, and they will thank you later for being persistent in teaching them good manners.

In this section, you will find tips and faux pas to help you to be more socially savvy, whether you are the parent doing the teaching or the young person growing up.

❀ "Manners for Minors"

❀ "Top Ten Car Pool Driver's Faux Pas"

❀ "Kids' Car Pool Faux Pas"

❀ "Children's Holiday Etiquette"—see page 70

❀ "Prom Etiquette for Young Ladies"

❀ "Prom Etiquette for Young Men"

❀ "Graduation Etiquette"

❀ "Top Ten Dorm Etiquette Tips"

Manners for Minors

Children pay more attention to what you do than to what you say. Start teaching your children manners from the time they are born, and you will not have to retrain them when they get older. Day by day, prepare them for adulthood.

Parents' Tips for Teaching Children

* Be consistent and persistent in teaching children manners. It is not a quick fix; it must become a habit.

* Incorporate the words "thank you" and "please" into children's vocabulary at a very early age.

* Teach your children the art of writing thank-you notes as soon as the child learns to write—never underestimate the power of a thank-you note.

* Practice meeting people by role-playing with your children beforehand.

* With your children, practice firmly shaking hands (web to web).

* Teach children dining basics at an early age, and help them continue to progress as they get older.

* Do not take them out to eat if they are not well-behaved in public. Keep working on it at home.

* Teach your children not only how to apologize, but also how to ask for forgiveness.

* Teach children to do random acts of kindness for family and friends.

* Do not criticize or embarrass children in front of their friends; it will scar them for life.

Set children up for success by setting expectations before you go into social situations.

Tips Children Should Know

❀ Treat others the way you want to be treated—when in doubt, always ask yourself, "How would I want to be treated?"

❀ Look people in the eye when shaking their hand or speaking to them—this shows your self-confidence.

❀ Learn how to give sincere compliments and how to gracefully receive a compliment. There is no need to contradict a compliment given to you—just smile and say, "thank you."

❀ Know that whining is not acceptable. Adults will be happy to listen to your request if you ask in a mannerly voice, not a whining voice.

❀ Speak politely and respectfully with adults.

At a minimum, children should be taught the basics.

Five manners children should know and practice by age five:

❀ Using table manners and using utensils correctly.

❀ Knowing the difference between their indoor voice and their outdoor voice.

❀ Shaking hands and looking people in the eyes when addressing them.

❀ Standing when being introduced and knowing when to say "thank you," "please," and "hello" when they see someone they know.

❀ Making their own bed.

Five more things (at a minimum) a child should add to his or her list by age ten:

❀ Carrying on a conversation with an adult and never interrupting others.

❀ Taking phone messages responsibly.

❀ Opening and holding doors for others.

❀ Staying organized and keeping track of their belongings.

❀ Writing thank-you notes for gifts or anything nice someone does.

Five more things a fifteen year-old should add to his or her list of manners:

❀ Initiating conversations with adults and making proper introductions.

❀ Being appreciative of others—without being reminded.

❀ Maintaining a list of responsibilities around the house.

❀ Understanding how to be a good houseguest and a good host.

❀ Communicating clearly and remaining comfortable in social situations.

> *The early years are the formative years, so do not wait until your children are teenagers before you start teaching them social skills.*

Top Ten Car Pool Driver's Faux Pas

Set a good example for your children, be considerate of others, and avoid these faux pas if you want to be a "good car pool parent."

1. Not buckling up! This goes for the driver as well as the children, even if you are "just going around the corner."

2. Arriving late to pick up children.

3. Stopping in the school's "moving traffic lane" to let children out of the car—causing them to run out in front of traffic.

4. Holding up the car pool line to take care of personal business such as talking to a teacher, putting backpacks in the trunk, or writing a last-minute note for your children to give to their teacher.

5. Leaving your car parked in the car pool line while you run in the school "for just a minute."

6. Not setting a good example by listening to inappropriate music, having inappropriate conversations, or using inappropriate language.

7. Running personal errands on the way home from carpool without checking with the other parents first.

8. Ignoring street signs (no U-turn, no left turn) near the school, and holding up traffic in the process.

9. Cutting in front of cars that arrived first in line—this can cause "line rage."

10. Not treating all children in the car pool equally (bringing drinks for your child and not offering drinks to others in the car).

Kids' Car Pool Faux Pas

The car pool line is no time to ease up on teaching our children manners. These are common faux pas committed by the car pool children.

Faux Pas

* Not being ready on time, and causing others to be late.

* Tracking muddy or wet shoes into the car.

* Not moving over, and forcing other children to climb over you and/or your belongings when they are getting into the car.

* Distractive behavior—being rowdy, yelling, bugging other children in the car.

* Making gestures at people in passing cars.

* Using inappropriate language or discussing inappropriate topics.

* Fighting—arguing over who gets dropped off first, who sits in the front seat, or which radio station to play.

* Eating in the car without permission from the driver, or leaving litter in the car pool car.

Children learn more from your actions than from your words. Set great examples for your children!

Prom Etiquette for Young Ladies

The prom is one of the most memorable events of high school. To be more at ease, follow these basic tips.

Tips

* Be an exceptional date on this night, even if he is not the date you dreamed of—it will be long remembered.

* Do not leave your date sitting alone at the table or on the dance floor by himself.

* Do not camp out in the ladies' room with your friends, chatting the night away.

* Buy a boutonniere for your date and pin it on his left lapel.

* Do not freak out if you show up in the same dress as someone else—simply compliment her on her good taste and get over it!

* Remember to always bring some cash—you never know when you will need it.

* Make sure your date knows what time your parents expect you home.

* Never be afraid to say no to alcohol, drugs, intimacy, or anything you feel uncomfortable doing.

* Remember that your date has probably spent much time and money on this event. Thank him for a wonderful evening.

* Do not chew gum (give it up at least for this one night).

* Smile and have fun!

Prom Etiquette for Young Men

Tips

* Check with your date to see what type of corsage she prefers. Ask the color of her dress in order to select a corsage that looks best. If you have no idea, just ask the florists for their recommendations. Do not hesitate to ask a parent to pin on the corsage if necessary. Remember, it is always worn on the left side.

* Dress appropriately. Do not embarrass your date and everyone else by dressing like a fool. Determine your dress attire and rent your tuxedo weeks in advance to be prepared.

* Make reservations ahead of time if you plan to take your date to dinner before the prom, but only after confirming plans with your date.

* Address your date's parents as Mr. and Mrs. unless you already have a close relationship with them.

* Always be on time, and make sure you know and respect your date's curfew.

* Be sociable with others at the prom, but make certain your date is the center of your attention.

* Determine how you will be arriving at the prom: limo, your parents, or perhaps your own car. If you choose your own car, clean it up, especially the inside.

❋ Please do not drink and drive.

❋ Do not use your cell phone while on your date. In fact, turn it off, or at least place it on silent.

❋ Remember your dining manners.

Graduation Etiquette

အါ

Twelve action-packed years of school are complete, and now it is time for your graduation, as well as all the parties and activities that go along with it. There are many details to be concerned with, along with many unanswered questions that arise on how to handle some basic situations. Read on and you will find out how to make the most of this very special event.

Tips

Invitations

* Distribute the graduation invitations only to close friends and family members, and send them at least two weeks prior to the ceremony.

* Send graduation announcements/invitations in two envelopes. The outer envelope should be personally addressed in blue or black ink.

* Use complete addresses with no abbreviations when addressing the envelopes. For example:

Mr. and Mrs. Charles S. Corbin and Family
2132 Singleton Avenue
Houston, Texas 75029

* Personally write the names of the recipients on the front of the inner envelope as if you were speaking to them. You should list children by name on the inner envelope only. For example:

Aunt Robin and Uncle Chuck
Allie and Reid

❀ Place the graduation announcement in the inner envelope with the front of the announcement facing the envelope flap.

Attire

❀ Wear the cap parallel to the ground, with the point of the cap between the eyes. The tassel hangs to your left and will be moved to the right upon graduation.

❀ Know the school dress customs, traditions, and expectations. You might need to wear a tie, and remember that shoes are just about the only part of the graduate's attire that is visible to the audience. Wear tasteful shoes—avoid flip-flops, sandals, tennis shoes, or bunny slippers!

❀ Avoid wearing dark clothes underneath a light-colored graduation gown. You might not even notice until the pictures are developed. Yikes!

❀ Encourage your guests to dress tastefully, and to dress for the weather, especially if the commencement is outdoors.

Graduation Gifts

❀ Graduate: Be sure to thank, with a handwritten note, everyone who sent a graduation gift. This note should simply acknowledge the gift, and should be sent immediately—however, if it takes you a month, a late note is better than no note!

❀ Guests: do not forget that gift giving is appropriate if you are invited to the graduation or to a party. If you are sent an announcement, it is not necessary to send a gift, but a graduation card is a nice gesture.

❊ Guests: Consider giving money. It is certainly an excellent gift to give to the graduate. Other appropriate gifts include luggage, a camera, jewelry, or gift certificates: these gifts should be mailed or given to the graduate as close to graduation day as possible. It is still acceptable to deliver gifts to the graduate up to two months afterward.

Bonus Tip for Graduate and Guests— Everyone, PLEASE silence your cell phones!

Top Ten Dorm Etiquette Tips

‮ﬧ‬

Moving away from home into a dorm and living with a new roommate is an enormous life change and will require a commitment of communication to make the experience an enjoyable one for all parties involved. Instead of learning these tips through the school of hard knocks, why not read them now and avoid the turbulence of a horrific roommate experience?

1. Ask before borrowing your roommate's belongings. If it is an emergency and you do use something that is not yours, let your roommate know as soon as possible; do not wait until he or she figures it out. What could be worse than seeing your roommate carrying your new Louis Vuitton handbag before you have had a chance to get it out of the dust bag?

2. Keep private information confidential. When you have a roommate, you will learn personal information that the rest of the world does not need to know. No one needs to know that your roommate has a mole the shape of Elvis on his back.

3. Be fair and share expenses. If you have agreed to share expenses, it is crucial to hold up your end of the bargain if you want to keep the roommate relationship harmonious.

4. Ask before you invite. Bringing a guest over unannounced is grounds for distress—a roommate is not always prepared for company. Always give as much notice as possible, even if it is only a few minutes.

5. Respect each other's schedule. If one roommate is trying to study while the other one is talking on the phone or watching television, it could cause a problem. It is essential to know each other's schedule and be extremely sensitive to it.

6. Clean up after yourself. Keep your personal area clean—especially when it comes to the common areas like the shower and the sink.

7. Take accurate phone messages and make sure your roommate gets the information. There is nothing worse than your parents showing up when the only one who knew about the visit was your roommate.

8. Keep your cell phone on "manner mode" during the night. Just because you are excited about a two a.m. call from "Mr. Right Now" does not mean the rest of the world wants to be awakened by an annoying ring.

9. Moving out of the way while others are getting off the dorm elevator, and waiting until everyone gets off before you enter shows respect. Moving to the back or side to create room for the next person is a must. Also, make sure the elevator is going in the direction you are headed before you get on, or it could be a very long ride.

10. Everyone needs space. Too much togetherness can cause unnecessary disagreements—a lot like marriage!

❧

Thank You

I want to extend a very heartfelt thank-you to an amazing team of individuals who helped in the creation and publication of my book....

My Husband and Partner
James Weaver

✿

Publisher
Brown Books

✿

Copy Editor
Deanne Dice

✿

Cover and Interior Design
David and Luke Edmonson
Ted Ruybal
Michael Turkett

✿

Photography
The best photographer in the world—
David Edmonson

✿

Public Relations
Robin Corbin

✿

Very Special Encouragement and Endorsement
Jean and Zig Ziglar